Snap books™

Fun Food for Cool Cooks

Apple Pie Calzones

AND OTHER COOKIE RECIPES

by Brekka Hervey Larrew

Capstone press®

Mankato, Minnesota

Snap Books are published by Capstone Press,
151 Good Counsel Drive, P.O. Box 669, Mankato, Minnesota 56002.
www.capstonepress.com

Library of Congress Cataloging-in-Publication Data
Larrew, Brekka Hervey.
    Apple pie calzones and other cookie recipes / by Brekka Hervey Larrew.
    p. cm. — (Snap books. Fun food for cool cooks)
    Summary: "Provides fun and unique recipes for cookies, including apple pie calzones,
rainbow braids, and peppermint drops. Includes easy instructions and a helpful tools glossary
with photos" — Provided by publisher.
    Includes bibliographical references and index.
    ISBN-13: 978-1-4296-1336-1 (hardcover)
    ISBN-10: 1-4296-1336-X (hardcover)
    1. Cookies — Juvenile literature. I. Title. II. Series.
TX772.L38 2008
641.8'654 — dc22   2007031424

Editors: Kathryn Clay and Christine Peterson
Designer: Juliette Peters
Photo Stylist: Kelly Garvin

Photo Credits:
All principle photography in this book by Capstone Press/Karon Dubke
Capstone Press/TJ Thoraldson Digital Photography, cooking utensils (all)
David Larrew, 32

Capstone Press thanks Pub 500 in Mankato, Minnesota, for assisting with photo shoots for this book.

1 2 3 4 5 6 13 12 11 10 09 08

TABLE OF CONTENTS

PAGE 10

PAGE 14

PAGE 16

PAGE 20

PAGE 22

PAGE 26

INTRODUCTION

SEEING STARS

When choosing a recipe, let the stars be your guide. Just follow this chart to find recipes that fit your cooking comfort level.

EASY: ★ ☆ ☆
MEDIUM: ★ ★ ☆
ADVANCED: ★ ★ ★

If you like cookies, then you'll agree that nothing beats homemade cookies. As the cookies bake, your home fills with wonderful smells. You can't wait to bite into a warm, soft cookie fresh from the oven.

Whether you like chocolate chips or fresh fruit, you'll find a fun recipe to satisfy your sweet tooth. These cookies taste so good, you'll want to share them with friends.

Is your mouth watering yet? Gather your ingredients. Your cookies will be ready in no time.

METRIC CONVERSION GUIDE

United States	Metric
¼ teaspoon	1.2 mL
½ teaspoon	2.5 mL
1 teaspoon	5 mL
1 tablespoon	15 mL
¼ cup	60 mL
⅓ cup	80 mL
½ cup	120 mL
⅔ cup	160 mL
¾ cup	175 mL
1 cup	240 mL
1 quart	1 liter

1 ounce	30 grams
2 ounces	55 grams
4 ounces	110 grams
½ pound	225 grams
1 pound	455 grams

Fahrenheit	Celsius
325°	160°
350°	180°
375°	190°
400°	200°
425°	220°
450°	230°

All good cooks know that a successful recipe takes a little preparation. Use this handy checklist to save time when working in the kitchen.

BEFORE YOU BEGIN

READ YOUR RECIPE

Once you've chosen a recipe, carefully read over it. The recipe will go smoothly if you understand the steps and techniques.

CHECK THE PANTRY

Make sure you have all the ingredients on hand. After all, it's hard to bake cookies without sugar!

DRESS FOR SUCCESS

Wear an apron to keep your clothes clean. Roll up long sleeves. Tie long hair back so it doesn't get in your way — or in the food.

GET OUT YOUR TOOLS

Sort through the cupboards and gather all the tools you'll need to prepare the recipe. Can't tell a spatula from a mixing spoon? No problem. Refer to the handy tools glossary in this book.

PREPARE YOUR INGREDIENTS

A little prep time at the start will pay off in the end.
- Rinse any fresh ingredients such as fruit and vegetables.
- Use a peeler to remove the peel from foods like apples and carrots.
- Cut up fresh ingredients as called for in the recipe. Keep an adult nearby when using a knife to cut or chop food.
- Measure all the ingredients and place them in separate bowls or containers so they're ready to use. Remember to use the correct measuring cups for dry and wet ingredients.

PREHEAT THE OVEN

If you're baking treats, it's important to preheat the oven. Cakes, cookies, and breads bake better in an oven that's heated to the correct temperature.

The kitchen may be unfamiliar turf for many young chefs. Here's a list of trusty tips to help keep you safe in the kitchen:

KITCHEN SAFETY

ADULT HELPERS

Ask an adult to help. Whether you're chopping, mixing, or baking, you'll want an adult nearby to lend a hand or answer questions.

FIRST AID

Keep a first aid kit handy in the kitchen, just in case you have an accident. A basic first aid kit contains bandages, a cream or spray to treat burns, alcohol wipes, gauze, and a small scissors.

WASH UP

Before starting any recipe, make sure to wash your hands. Wash your hands again after working with messy ingredients like jelly or syrup.

HANDLE HABITS

Turn handles of cooking pots toward the center of the stove. You don't want anyone to bump into a handle that's sticking off the stove.

USING KNIVES

It's always best to get an adult's help when using knives. Choose a knife that's the right size for both your hands and the food. It may be tough to cut carrots with a paring knife that's too small. Hold the handle firmly when cutting, and keep your fingers away from the blade.

COVER UP

Always wear oven mitts or use pot holders to take hot trays and pans out of the oven.

KEEP IT CLEAN

Spills and drips are bound to happen in the kitchen. Wipe up messes with a paper towel or clean kitchen towel to keep your workspace clean.

Give the all-American apple pie an Italian twist with this cookie recipe. With a sugar cookie crust, this turnover is a perfect pizza party dessert.

DIFFICULTY LEVEL: ★ ★ ☆
MAKES: 2 DOZEN COOKIES
PREHEAT OVEN: 350° FAHRENHEIT

APPLE PIE CALZONE COOKIES

WHAT YOU NEED

●● Ingredients

1 Granny Smith apple, peeled
1 tablespoon butter
1 tablespoon sugar
½ teaspoon cinnamon
¼ teaspoon nutmeg
⅓ cup flour
1 (16.5-18 ounce) package refrigerated
   sugar cookie dough
½ teaspoon cinnamon
1½ tablespoons sugar

●● Tools

cutting board   paring knife   saucepan   colander

microwave-safe
bowl   rolling mat   rolling pin

3-inch round
cookie cutter   baking sheet   tablespoon

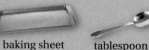

small bowl   oven mitt   pot holder

1 On a cutting board, slice a peeled apple into fourths with a paring knife. Cut out the core and dice apple into small chunks.

2 Place the apple in a small saucepan and cover with water. Cook over medium heat until soft. Drain apples in a colander and set them aside to dry.

3 Microwave butter in a microwave-safe bowl for 15 seconds. Add sugar, cinnamon, nutmeg, and apples. Stir mixture until combined.

4 Dust rolling mat and rolling pin with flour. Use the rolling pin to flatten cookie dough until it is ½-inch thick. Cut out dough with a cookie cutter. Place cookies on an ungreased baking sheet, about 2 inches apart.

5 Spoon 1 tablespoon of the apple mixture into the center of each cookie. Fold the cookie in half and press the edges together. Refrigerate for 1 hour before baking.

6 In a small bowl, mix ½ teaspoon cinnamon and 1½ tablespoons sugar. Sprinkle on cookies.

7 Bake for 12–18 minutes. Use an oven mitt or pot holder to remove baking sheet from the oven.

Let's Roll!

Rolling cookie dough can be tricky and sticky. The key to rolling dough is having plenty of flour in all the right places. First, cover the rolling pin and rolling surface with a thin layer of flour. Place your cookie dough in the middle of the floured surface. Sprinkle more flour on top of the dough. Be sure to add more flour every time you roll out the dough.

Tasty Tip

Try making caramel apple calzones. Just drizzle some caramel ice cream topping on the cookies before serving.

DIFFICULTY LEVEL: ★ ★ ☆
MAKES: 4 DOZEN COOKIES
PREHEAT OVEN: 350° FAHRENHEIT

Sugar, Spice, and Everything Nice Cookies

WHAT YOU NEED

Ingredients

2 cups brown sugar
1 teaspoon vanilla
    extract
½ cup oil
2 eggs
1 (5-ounce) can
    evaporated milk
3½ cups flour
1 teaspoon baking soda
1 teaspoon cinnamon
½ teaspoon nutmeg
½ teaspoon salt

1 cup chocolate chips
¾ cup toffee chips
¾ cup chopped pecans
½ teaspoon cinnamon
2 teaspoons sugar

Tools

large mixing bowl

rubber scraper   small bowl

small mixing bowl   baking sheet   oven mitt

pot holder

nonstick cooking spray

1 In a large mixing bowl, combine brown sugar, vanilla, and oil with a rubber scraper.

2 Crack eggs into a small bowl and throw shells away. Add eggs to the large mixing bowl. Add evaporated milk and mix together with the rubber scraper.

3 In a small mixing bowl, mix together flour, baking soda, cinnamon, nutmeg, and salt. Add these ingredients to the large mixing bowl and mix well with the rubber scraper.

4 Add chocolate chips, toffee chips, and chopped pecans to the dough and stir.

5 Spray a baking sheet evenly with nonstick cooking spray. Place 1-inch balls of dough on the baking sheet, about 2 inches apart.

6 In a small bowl, mix ½ teaspoon cinnamon with 2 teaspoons sugar. Sprinkle mixture onto dough.

7 Bake for 8–10 minutes. Use an oven mitt or pot holder to remove baking sheet from the oven.

Cool Tips For Hot Cookies

• Follow directions carefully. When baking, it is very important to add the ingredients in the proper order.

• Don't overstir the dough or you'll end up with flat, tough cookies.

• Place one baking sheet in the oven at a time so the cookies will brown evenly.

• Use a timer so your cookies don't burn.

11

Peanut butter and jelly sandwiches have been lunchbox favorites since the 1940s. Now you can enjoy a PB & J for dessert. Your classmates will be lining up to trade lunches.

DIFFICULTY LEVEL: ★ ★ ☆
MAKES: 2 DOZEN COOKIES
PREHEAT OVEN: 375° FAHRENHEIT

PEANUT BUTTER SANDWICH COOKIES

WHAT YOU NEED

● ● *Ingredients*

1½ cups flour
½ teaspoon salt
1 teaspoon baking powder
¾ cup butter (1½ sticks)
½ cup creamy peanut butter
½ cup sugar
½ cup light brown sugar (firmly packed)
½ teaspoon vanilla extract
1 large egg
2 tablespoons sugar
1½ cups jelly (any flavor)

● ● *Tools*

small mixing bowl   rubber scraper   large mixing bowl

baking sheet   tablespoon   small bowl   fork

oven mitt   pot holder   spatula

wire cooling rack

1 In a small mixing bowl, stir flour, salt, and baking powder with a rubber scraper. Set this bowl aside.

2 In a large mixing bowl, mix butter, peanut butter, sugar, brown sugar, and vanilla. Crack an egg into a small bowl and throw shells away. Add egg to the large mixing bowl. Stir together with the rubber scraper.

3 Add dry ingredients to the large mixing bowl and stir together.

4 Place 1-inch balls of dough on an ungreased baking sheet, about 2 inches apart.

5 Put 2 tablespoons sugar into a small bowl. Use a fork dipped in the sugar to form a crisscross pattern on top of each cookie.

6 Bake for 9–11 minutes. Use an oven mitt or pot holder to remove baking sheet from oven. With a spatula, place cookies on a wire cooling rack.

7 When cookies have cooled, spread jelly onto the bottom of a cookie. Place a second cookie on top of the jelly to form a sandwich.

Popular PB & J

Peanut butter and jelly sandwiches are popular with the young and old alike. But how did this tasty combo get its start? During World War II (1939–1945), U.S. soldiers were given both peanut butter and jelly as part of their rations. Historians believe soldiers added jelly to their peanut butter to make it taste better. When the soldiers returned home, sales of peanut butter and jelly soared. The rest is history!

Need a new way to enjoy a banana split? Try a banana split cookie topped with frosting, peanuts, and a cherry. Just like the ice cream version, these cookies will melt in your mouth!

DIFFICULTY LEVEL: ★ ★ ☆
MAKES: 4 DOZEN COOKIES
PREHEAT OVEN: 375° FAHRENHEIT

BANANA SPLIT COOKIES

WHAT YOU NEED

•• *Ingredients*

½ cup (1 stick) butter, softened
1 cup brown sugar, firmly packed
2 ripe bananas
2 eggs
2 cups flour
2 teaspoons baking powder
¼ teaspoon baking soda

¼ teaspoon salt
¼ teaspoon nutmeg
½ teaspoon cinnamon
1 (16-ounce) can cream cheese frosting
1 (10-ounce) jar of cherries
1 (2-ounce) package chopped peanuts

•• *Tools*

large mixing bowl   rubber scraper   small bowl

fork   small mixing bowl   baking sheet

oven mitt   pot holder

plastic wrap
nonstick cooking spray

1 In a large mixing bowl, cream butter and brown sugar with a rubber scraper.

2 Peel bananas and place them in a small bowl. Use a fork to mash bananas until they form a smooth paste. Add to the large mixing bowl.

3 Crack eggs into the small bowl and throw shells away. Add eggs to the large mixing bowl. Mix ingredients with the rubber scraper.

4 In a small mixing bowl, combine flour, baking powder, baking soda, salt, nutmeg, and cinnamon. Add this to the large bowl and mix together. Cover bowl with plastic wrap and refrigerate for 1 hour.

5 Spray baking sheet with nonstick cooking spray. Place 2-inch balls of dough on baking sheet, about 2 inches apart.

6 Bake for 8–10 minutes. Use an oven mitt or pot holder to remove baking sheet from oven. Allow cookies to cool.

7 Spread frosting on each cookie. Top each cookie with a cherry and chopped peanuts.

Crunch!

A crunchy cookie can be good, but not when that crunch comes from a piece of eggshell. To keep your cookies shell-free, first crack your eggs into a small bowl. Then pour the eggs into the mixing bowl with the other ingredients.

Trusty Tip

Many cookie recipes begin by asking you to cream the butter and sugar. By mixing these ingredients until smooth, you form air bubbles in the dough. Add baking soda or baking powder, and these bubbles will grow while baking. This will make your cookies light and fluffy.

Do you ever feel like you have two personalities? Some days you feel friendly. Other times you're shy. These cookies celebrate our many moods and tastes with two different flavors in each cookie.

DIFFICULTY LEVEL: ★ ★ ★
MAKES: 2 DOZEN COOKIES
PREHEAT OVEN: 350° FAHRENHEIT

YIN AND YANG COOKIES

WHAT YOU NEED

●● Ingredients

1 (16.5-18 ounce) package refrigerated sugar cookie dough
1 (16.5-18 ounce) package refrigerated gingerbread dough
¼ cup flour (for dusting)
1½ tablespoons chocolate chips
1½ tablespoons white chocolate chips

●● Tools

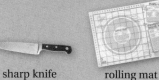

cutting board   sharp knife   rolling mat

rolling pin   baking sheet   oven mitt

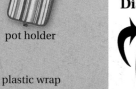

pot holder

plastic wrap

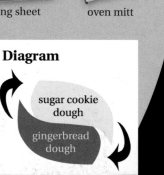

Diagram

sugar cookie dough

gingerbread dough

1 On a cutting board, roll out cookie dough and cut each roll in half lengthwise with a sharp knife.

2 Dust the rolling mat and rolling pin with flour. Place one half of dough on the dusted surface. Roll the dough into a 3-inch wide wedge shape (¾-inch thick on one side and ¼-inch thick on the other). Repeat with the second roll of dough.

3 Stack together one wedge of each flavor so that the thin edges are on opposite sides and extend past the large wedge of dough.

4 Wrap the thin edges around the dough to form a tube with the two flavors (see diagram). Roll dough in plastic wrap and refrigerate for 1 hour.

5 Remove dough from refrigerator. Use the knife to cut ½-inch slices of dough. Place on an ungreased baking sheet, about 2 inches apart.

6 Add a chocolate chip to the sugar cookie dough and a white chocolate chip to the gingerbread dough. Bake according to package directions. Use an oven mitt or pot holder to remove baking sheet from oven.

16

Yin and Yang

In the western world, some people believe yin and yang stand for evil and good. But yin and yang aren't that simple. Yin represents the darker side of things, while yang represents the lighter side. These opposites need each other in order to balance. There would be no day without night, and there would be no joy without sadness.

Tasty Tip

Instead of gingerbread dough, try using peanut butter or chocolate dough.

You don't need a campfire to enjoy a s'more. These cookies combine the s'more flavor with a peanut butter twist. So whether you're camping outdoors or in, these cookies make a sweet snack.

DIFFICULTY LEVEL: ★ ☆ ☆
MAKES: 2 DOZEN COOKIES
PREHEAT OVEN: 325° FAHRENHEIT

PEANUT BUTTER S'MORE BITES

WHAT YOU NEED

●● *Ingredients*

1½ cups creamy peanut butter
¾ cup milk chocolate chips
1½ cups graham cracker crumbs
1 (14-ounce) can sweetened condensed milk
1 cup mini marshmallows

●● *Tools*

large mixing bowl

rubber scraper

small bowl

baking sheet

oven mitt

pot holder

nonstick cooking spray

1 In a large mixing bowl, combine peanut butter, chocolate chips, and 1 cup graham cracker crumbs with a rubber scraper.

2 Add the sweetened condensed milk and mix with the rubber scraper.

3 Form 2-inch balls of dough. Press 3 or 4 mini marshmallows into each ball. Pinch dough so that it completely covers the marshmallows.

4 Place the remaining graham cracker crumbs into a small bowl. Roll each ball in the graham cracker crumbs.

5 Spray baking sheet with nonstick cooking spray. Place dough onto cookie sheet, about 2 inches apart.

6 Bake for 15 minutes. Use an oven mitt or pot holder to remove baking sheet from oven.

Variation

For a more chewy cookie, substitute ½ large marshmallow for the mini marshmallows.

Trusty Tip

Rather than buy graham cracker crumbs, you can make your own. All you need are graham crackers, a zip-top plastic bag, and a rolling pin. Put the crackers in the bag. Use a rolling pin to smash the crackers until they become small crumbs.

It's hard not to stop and stare at a rainbow. The same goes for these colorful cookie braids. And there's a bonus: these cookies taste as good as they look!

DIFFICULTY LEVEL: ★ ★ ★
MAKES: 2 DOZEN COOKIES
PREHEAT OVEN: 400° FAHRENHEIT

SUGARY RAINBOW BRAIDS

WHAT YOU NEED

●● *Ingredients*

1½ cups sugar
¾ cup (1½ sticks) butter, softened
2 eggs
1 teaspoon vanilla extract
1 tablespoon milk
3 cups flour
2 teaspoons baking powder
½ teaspoon salt
red, yellow, and blue food coloring
sugar sprinkles

●● *Tools*

large mixing bowl

rubber scraper

small bowl

small mixing bowl

baking sheet

oven mitt

pot holder

3 bowls
plastic wrap
wax paper

1 In a large mixing bowl, cream together sugar and butter with a rubber scraper.

2 Crack eggs into a small bowl and throw away shells. Add eggs, vanilla, and milk to the large mixing bowl.

3 In a small mixing bowl, combine flour, baking powder, and salt. Gradually add these to the large bowl and mix together.

4 Divide dough into three equal sections and place into separate bowls. Add 3 or 4 drops of food coloring to each bowl. Mix dough and food coloring. Cover the bowls with plastic wrap and refrigerate for 1 hour.

5 Form 1-inch balls of dough. Roll each ball into a rope that is 5 or 6 inches long.

6 Place three ropes (one of each color) on wax paper. Braid ropes together (see sidebar). Repeat with the remaining ropes.

7 Place each braid on an ungreased baking sheet, about 3 inches apart. Top with sugar sprinkles.

8 Bake for 7–9 minutes. Use an oven mitt or pot holder to remove baking sheet from oven.

Mix It Up

Rather than plain sugar cookies, you can make dough flavored with peppermint, coconut, banana, or orange. You could even braid two or three flavors together. Instead of vanilla flavoring, add ½ teaspoon of a different flavored extract to each dough.

Braiding Tips

To make braids, put three ropes of dough next to each other. Take the right rope and move it over the middle rope. Take the left rope and move it to the middle. Repeat until braid is complete.

Double your fun by baking with brown and white chocolate!
Adding white chocolate chips to these chewy brownie cookies
creates a fun polka dot treat.

DIFFICULTY LEVEL: ★ ☆ ☆
MAKES: 2 DOZEN COOKIES
PREHEAT OVEN: 375° FAHRENHEIT

POLKA DOT BROWNIE BURSTS

WHAT YOU NEED

●● *Ingredients*

⅔ cup vegetable shortening
1 cup light brown sugar, firmly packed
1 tablespoon water
½ tablespoon vanilla extract
2 eggs
1¾ cups flour
⅓ cup cocoa
½ teaspoon baking soda
½ teaspoon salt
2 cups white chocolate chips

●● *Tools*

large mixing bowl

rubber scraper

small bowl

small mixing bowl

baking sheet

oven mitt

pot holder

1 In a large mixing bowl, combine shortening, brown sugar, water, and vanilla with a rubber scraper.

2 Crack the eggs into a small bowl and throw shells away. Add the eggs to the large bowl one at a time.

3 In a small mixing bowl, combine flour, cocoa, baking soda, and salt. Gradually add the dry ingredients to the large mixing bowl. Stir with the rubber scraper until all ingredients are blended.

4 Add 1¼ cup white chocolate chips to the dough and mix well.

5 Place 1-inch balls of dough onto an ungreased baking sheet, about 2 inches apart. Press 5 or 6 white chocolate chips, flat side facing up, into each cookie.

6 Bake for 8–10 minutes. Do not overbake. Use an oven mitt or pot holder to remove baking sheet from oven.

Not Chocolate?

Ever wonder why white chocolate tastes different from regular chocolate? White chocolate does contain cocoa butter, but it's not really chocolate. All chocolate contains chocolate liquor, a substance that is produced in cocoa beans. White chocolate does not contain this ingredient, so it isn't really chocolate — but it is delicious!

Butterscotch Lollipop Cookies combine two favorites — cookies and candy. You'll enjoy chewing the cookie and licking the lollipop. Arrange in a colorful box, and you've got a tasty gift to share.

DIFFICULTY LEVEL: ★ ★ ★
MAKES: 2 DOZEN COOKIES
PREHEAT OVEN: 350° FAHRENHEIT

BUTTERSCOTCH LOLLIPOP COOKIES

WHAT YOU NEED

Ingredients

25 butterscotch hard candies
½ cup (1 stick) butter, softened
½ cup brown sugar, firmly packed
1 (4-ounce) package cook-and-serve
    butterscotch pudding
1 egg
1½ cups flour
½ teaspoon baking soda
⅓ cup flour (for dusting)
yellow sugar sprinkles

Tools

baking sheet

rolling pin

large mixing bowl

rubber scraper

rolling mat

3-inch round
cookie cutter

1½-inch round
cookie cutter

spatula

small wooden
craft sticks

oven mitt

pot holder

aluminum foil
zip-top bag

1 Line a baking sheet with aluminum foil. Place candies into a zip-top bag and crush with a rolling pin. Set aside.

2 In a large mixing bowl, cream together butter and brown sugar with a rubber scraper. Stir in dry pudding mix.

3 Add egg, flour, and baking soda and stir until mixture becomes a stiff dough. Form dough into a ball.

4 Dust a rolling mat and rolling pin with flour. Place dough ball on the rolling mat. Use a rolling pin to flatten dough to ¼-inch thick.

5 Cut out cookies with a 3-inch cookie cutter. Use a 1½-inch cookie cutter to cut a hole in each cookie.

6 Using a spatula, place a cookie on the baking sheet. Press a craft stick into the edge of the cookie. Press a second cookie over the first cookie, covering the stick.

7 Fill the hole in each cookie with crushed candies. Sprinkle the cookies with yellow sugar sprinkles.

8 Bake for 12 minutes. Use an oven mitt or pot holder to remove baking sheet from oven. Allow cookies to cool until the melted candy has hardened (about 20 minutes). Gently peel cookies from foil.

Cut It Out!

Don't have cookie cutters at home? No problem. Many everyday kitchen items can be used to cut cookie dough. Drink glasses and empty tin cans work great to cut cookies into a circular shape. Just be sure any object you use is clean.

25

Coated with powdered sugar to look like snowballs, these peppermint drops make the perfect holiday treat. After a day out in the snow, try a few cookies with a mug of hot chocolate.

DIFFICULTY LEVEL: ★ ★ ☆
MAKES: 3 DOZEN COOKIES
PREHEAT OVEN: 350° FAHRENHEIT

SNOWY PEPPERMINT DROPS

WHAT YOU NEED

● ● Ingredients

10 peppermint candies
1 cup butter, softened
1 teaspoon peppermint extract
2 cups flour
½ cup sugar
¼ teaspoon salt
1 cup powdered sugar

● ● Tools

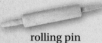
rolling pin

large mixing bowl

rubber scraper

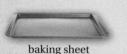
baking sheet

oven mitt

pot holder

small bowl

wire cooling rack

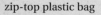
zip-top plastic bag

1 Place peppermint candies into a large zip-top plastic bag. Crush them with a rolling pin so they have a powdery texture and set aside.

2 In a large mixing bowl, cream together butter and peppermint extract with a rubber scraper. Stir crushed candy into the mixture.

3 Add flour, sugar, and salt to butter mixture and stir well. Place the dough into the zip-top bag and seal. Refrigerate for 1 hour.

4 Place 1-inch balls of dough onto an ungreased baking sheet, about 2 inches apart.

5 Bake for 10–12 minutes. Use an oven mitt or pot holder to remove baking sheet from oven. Allow cookies to cool for 5 minutes.

6 Put powdered sugar in a small bowl. Place cookies into the bowl and cover with powdered sugar. Set cookies on a wire cooling rack for 10 minutes. Cover the cookies with powdered sugar again.

Tasty Tip

To make peppermint thumbprints, add this easy filling:

In a small bowl, mix 2 tablespoons softened cream cheese, 2 teaspoons milk, ⅓ cup powdered sugar, and five crushed peppermint candies with a spoon. Use your thumb to make a "thumbprint" bowl in each ball of dough. Spoon ½ teaspoon of filling into each thumbprint. Bake as directed.

TOOLS GLOSSARY

baking sheet — a flat metal tray used for baking foods

colander — a bowl-shaped strainer used for washing or draining food

cookie cutter — a hollow shape made from metal or plastic that is used to cut cookie dough

cutting board — a wooden or plastic board used when slicing or chopping foods

fork — an eating utensil often used to stir or mash

microwave-safe bowl — a non-metal bowl used in microwave ovens

mixing bowl — a sturdy bowl used for mixing ingredients

oven mitt — a large mitten made from heavy fabric used to protect hands when removing hot pans from the oven

paring knife — a small, sharp knife used for peeling or slicing

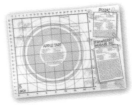

pot holder — a thick, heavy fabric cut into a square or circle that is used to remove hot pans from an oven

rolling mat — a flat, plastic surface used when rolling out dough

rolling pin — a cylinder-shaped tool used to flatten dough

rubber scraper — a kitchen tool with a rubber paddle on the end

small bowl — a bowl used for mixing a small amount of ingredients

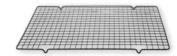

wire cooling rack — a rectangular rack that allows baked goods to cool quickly and evenly

saucepan — a deep pot with a handle

spatula — a kitchen tool with a broad, flat metal or plastic blade at the end, used for removing food from pans

wooden craft sticks — small, flat sticks with rounded ends

sharp knife — a kitchen knife with long blade used to cut ingredients

tablespoon — an eating utensil often used to stir or scoop

GLOSSARY

cream (KREEM) — to mix ingredients until soft and smooth

dice (DISSE) — to cut something into cubes

dust (DUHST) — to lightly sprinkle

extract (EK-strakt) — a strong solution of liquid made from plant juice; vanilla extract is made from vanilla beans.

filling (FIL-ing) — the food inside a sandwich, pie, cookie, or cake

ration (RASH-uhn) — a soldier's daily share of food

turnover (turn-OH-vur) — a baked pastry in which half of the crust is folded on top of the filling and sealed shut

wedge (WEJ) — a piece of food that is thin at one end and thick at the other, like a slice of pie

READ MORE

Devins, Susan. *Christmas Cookies: A Holiday Cookbook.* Cambridge, Mass.: Candlewick Press, 2007.

Dunnington, Rose. *Greatest Cookies Ever: Dozens of Delicious, Chewy, Chunky, Fun & Foolproof Recipes.* New York: Lark Books, 2005.

MacLeod, Elizabeth. *Bake and Make Amazing Cookies.* Kids Can Do It. Tonawanda, N.Y.: Kids Can Press, 2004.

INTERNET SITES

FactHound offers a safe, fun way to find Internet sites related to this book. All of the sites on FactHound have been researched by our staff.

Here's how:
1. Visit *www.facthound.com*
2. Choose your grade level.
3. Type in this book ID **142961336X** for age-appropriate sites. You may also browse subjects by clicking on letters, or by clicking on pictures and words.
4. Click on the **Fetch It** button.

FactHound will fetch the best sites for you!

ABOUT THE AUTHOR

Brekka Hervey Larrew began cooking with her mother when she was a child, mainly because she loved to eat (and still does). As a teenager, she held elaborate seven-course dinner parties for friends and relatives. Larrew baked as many varieties of cookies as she could find in recipe books. She has experimented with multicultural cooking and has worked to perfect the art of baking pies.

Larrew taught elementary and middle school for 12 years. Currently she stays home with her two children, both of whom help out in the kitchen. She lives in Nashville, Tennessee.

INDEX